Dr. Fry's

Pocket Charts

Effective
Ideas
and
Activities

by Edward Fry, Ph.D.

Teacher Created Materials, Inc.
6421 Industry Way
Westminster, CA 92683
www.teachercreated.com

ISBN-0-7439-3522-5

©2003 by Teacher Created Materials, Inc.
Made in U.S.A.

Table of Contents

Table of Contents

Preface

Pocket charts are not new teaching tools. They are time tested and have proven useful in thousands of classrooms and tutoring situations. That is what is so good about them.

Pocket charts are, however, not used enough. This book will show you many different ways you can effectively teach using pocket charts. They are frequently used in teaching beginning reading, and that is an important use which shall be discussed first. But pocket charts can also be used to teach math, spelling, and vocabulary improvement.

When teaching reading, pocket charts can effectively help you teach phonics, sight words, phonograms, and picture nouns. Using slightly more advanced chart contents can help you teach phrases, sentence patterns, spelling, and grammar.

Unfortunately, pocket charts are often thought of as a teaching tool mainly for primary grade levels 1 and 2. This is, indeed, unfortunate because they are equally valuable in preschool and kindergarten and also in the upper grades.

Nearly all of the lessons and content in this book are suitable for remedial instruction with older students or for students who are English Language Learners (ELL).

So, open your eyes and open your mind. Whether you are a beginning teacher or one with many years of experience, I think you will get some new ideas on the effective use of pocket charts.

Edward Fry, Ph.D.

Section 1

Teaching Methods

Basic Questions

What is a pocket chart?

A pocket chart is usually a large board or piece of cardboard with several rows or slots into which cards can be inserted. For example, several word cards or flashcards can be inserted in a row to form a phrase or sentence. The teacher can easily add, change, or take out word cards.

Basic Questions

Do you need a pocket chart to use the methods discussed in this book?

No. The same techniques work quite well by displaying cards in other ways, such as standing them up along the bottom of a chalkboard or even laying them flat on a table.

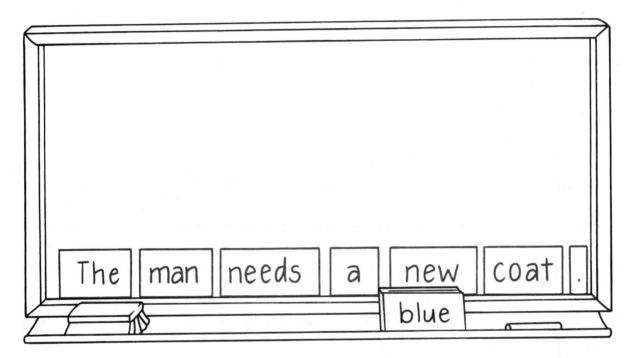

The | man | needs | a | new | coat | .

blue

Cards on Chalkboard

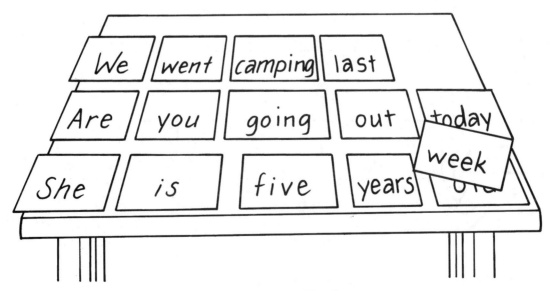

We | went | camping | last

Are | you | going | out | today

She | is | five | years | week

Cards on Table

Do I need commercially-prepared cards or can I make my own?

Both have advantages; in fact, many teachers use both.

Commercially-made word cards have bold, neat print and are ready to use, saving teacher-preparation time. The commercially-made cards have a carefully selected and often research-based curriculum. This book will give you much of the same content, however, if you wish to make your own. The pages in the back of the book (pages 63–96) can easily be duplicated and made into cards.

Teacher-made cards are inexpensive and easy to make. Just cut up tagboard and write with a bold, felt-tip pen. An advantage of teacher-made cards is that they can reflect exactly what is going on in the classroom. For example, the teacher can use the name of a character in a story that the class is currently reading.

Commerically-made Cards

Teacher-made Cards

Basic Reading Lesson

One traditional method of using a pocket chart to teach reading is for the teacher to select a few words and place them in the chart. The words may form a short sentence or phrase.

The teacher reads the words to the students, a small group of students reads them together, and then each child takes a turn reading the words. The teacher can then add more words or sentences. For content, see the Instant Words on pages 48–53 and the Picture Nouns on pages 63–82.

There are some different ways to teach the basic reading lesson.

- **Variation 1**
  A student acts as teacher.

- **Variation 2**
  The teacher points to words out of order.

- **Variation 3**
  A bit of a game format is used in which the first student to call out the word gets a point.

- **Variation 4**
  The teacher substitutes one word or a rebus (picture) in the sentence.

There are also different ways to follow up with the basic reading lesson.

- **Follow-up 1**
  The students write (copy) the words on the chart.

- **Follow-up 2**
  Leave the chart up all day so students can see it and try reading it on their own or with a friend.

- **Follow-up 3**
  Repeat the same lesson the next day; then add more words or a different sentence.

Caution: Keep the lessons short and simple so that most of the students achieve success. Increase difficulty and new content gradually.

Concepts

The Basic Reading Lesson on page 9 might look rather simple but there are some underlying concepts that are being taught. Without these fundamental concepts, it is very difficult—if not impossible—for anyone to learn to read.

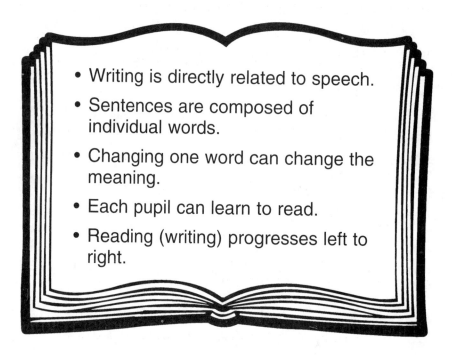

- Writing is directly related to speech.
- Sentences are composed of individual words.
- Changing one word can change the meaning.
- Each pupil can learn to read.
- Reading (writing) progresses left to right.

Teaching Tips: The Basic Reading Lesson gives you a great opportunity to heap praise on each student.

Let each slower student handle the cards and trace the letters with his or her finger while saying the word.

Alphabet

Learning the Alphabet

Pocket charts are effective tools for teaching the alphabet. One of their virtues is that they allow you to present as few or as many letters as you wish in a lesson. You can present single letters, then combine them to show how a word is formed. Beginning students need two alphabet skills: (1) how to read the letters (i.e., say the letter name) and (2) how to write the letter. These two skills are often taught together.

In order to do these alphabet-learning lessons, you will need a set of cards that has a single letter on each card. If you make your own cards, start by putting a capital letter on each card. If you use the commercially-prepared alphabet cards from Teacher Created Materials, you will note that there is a capital letter on one side of a card and the lowercase letter on the back side.

For a beginning lesson, start by putting three or four capital letter cards up on the chart. Tell the students the names of the letters and ask the students to read them back. Give each student a turn to say the letter names.

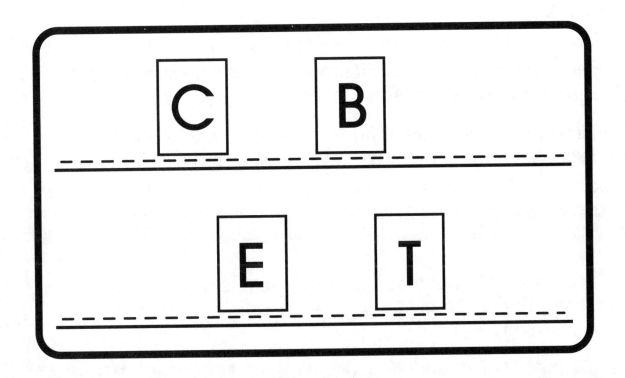

Alphabet

Learning the Alphabet *(cont.)*

There are some ways to vary the alphabet lesson.

- **Variation 1**

  Mix up the order of the letters and see if the students can still read them.

- **Variation 2**

  Add more letters.

- **Variation 3**

  Add lowercase letters.

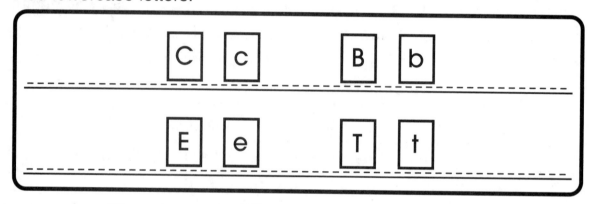

There are also different ways to follow up the alphabet lesson.

- **Follow-up 1**

  Have the students copy (write) the letters. Be sure that they are using the proper strokes (direction of moving the pencil when writing the letter). See the letters on pages 91–96.

- **Follow-up 2**

  Photocopy a page from a book or other printed material. Have the students point to the letter(s) taught in the lesson, or have the students circle all the *M*'s, for example.

> **Caution: Do not teach too many letters at once. Teach only a few. Be guided by the students' successful rate of learning.**

Alphabet

Alphabetical Order

It is important for many reasons to know alphabetical order. For example, students will need to know it to look up words in a dictionary or an index. Alphabetical order is like an alternative numbering system used for filing, outlines, and listing all sorts of things like names in the telephone book, and also finding a book in a library.

You can use pocket charts to teach alphabetical order much like you teach learning letter names or the basic reading lesson. Display a few alphabet letter cards, and call attention to the order. Mix up the cards, and ask the students to put them back in order.

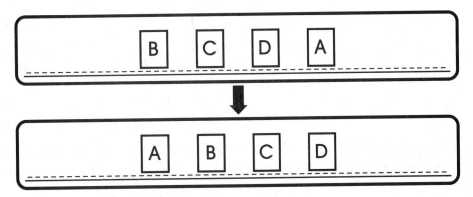

There are ways to vary the lesson on alphabetical order.

- **Variation 1**

  Add more letters.

- **Variation 2**

  Make a game of seeing who can do it quickest or first.

- **Variation 3**

  Learn the alphabet song. Use it to help the students put the letters in order.

There are different ways to follow up on the alphabetical order lesson.

- **Follow-up 1**

  Have a small group of toys, objects, pictures, or word cards and ask the students put them in alphabetical order.

- **Follow-up 2**

  Show the students various places where alphabetical order is used, such as a dictionary or their names in a roll book.

Alphabet

Handwriting

Teaching handwriting frequently occurs at the same time as learning to read the alphabet, and the two make a good combination. There are a number of good handwriting styles. Some examples are on pages 91–96.

A pocket chart can be a great help in teaching handwriting. It can show just one or a few letters at a time for the students to practice. Letters can be left up for the students to copy during the lesson. In fact, they can be left up all day or for several days for students to refer back to.

Some letter cards, like *Dr. Fry's Alphabet Flashcards* and the cards on pages 91–96, have stroking arrows on them to facilitate learning how to write each letter. Stroking arrows tell the student which stroke to make first, like the downward straight line in making the letter *B*. Teacher-made letter cards can include stroking arrows also.

The students' learning of proper letter formation can be aided by use of lined primary paper which shows the top, bottom, and middle lines for forming letters.

The teacher can have students practice writing just a few letters at a time. For young and slower students, let the students trace with their finger the stroking on the letter cards.

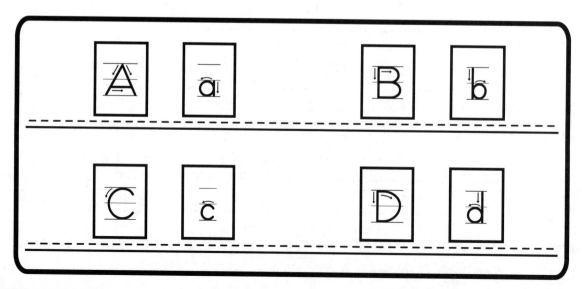

Spelling

Beginning Spelling

As soon as you start teaching the alphabet (letter names), your pupils will want to start writing words. In fact, even before you teach beginning handwriting, your pupils will have experimented with make-believe writing, scribbling, and invented handwriting (an approximation of real handwriting).

Learning to spell is a lifelong process. This book on pocket charts will address it many ways, but here are some suggestions for the very beginning. You might start with some Picture Nouns (pages 63–82) so students can quickly get the connection between a group of letters and a pictograph (drawing or photo). For example, you might take the following three letter cards: *m*, *a*, and *n*. Put them all together and tell the students that they spell *man*. You might also have a card with a pictograph or a stick figure and place it alongside of the word *man*. Scramble the letters *anm* and say it is not a word. Next, have a student try to place the letters back in the correct order. Let the students read the word—first, with the picture card alongside and then with the picture card taken away. Next, mix the letters again but differently than the first time so students are not just memorizing the order. Then, repeat the process again. Add another Picture Noun when the students are comfortable with the first word.

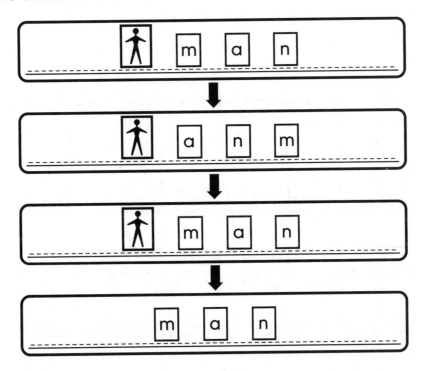

Spelling

Beginning Spelling *(cont.)*

You can use any noun that is easy to illustrate, but here are a few with easy spelling:

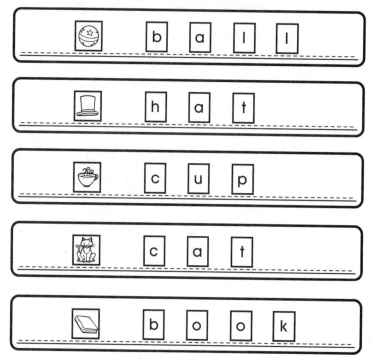

Copy the Picture Nouns on pages 63–82, make your own, or use commercially-prepared flashcards.

- **Follow-up 1**

  Repeat the reading of the words the next day.

- **Follow-up 2**

  Have the students copy the words from the pocket chart.

- **Follow-up 3**

  See if students can write the words from memory or spell them orally.

Caution: Praise the students for spelling the words correctly or almost correctly. Don't demand perfection.

Spelling

Advanced Spelling

The pages on Beginning Spelling (pages 15 and 16) highlighted the initial concept of spelling, namely that words are composed of individual letters and you have to use the right letters in the right order. What we refer to as "real spelling" is the kind of spelling lessons used throughout elementary school. This can be formal (using a spelling series or set curriculum) or informal (such as incidental words the teacher selects from errors in student-written stories).

Pocket charts can be used to aid both formal and informal spelling instruction. For example, the teacher can display word cards for all words, or just the more difficult words, from the spelling lesson. The word cards can be the whole word or single letters spelling out the word. If the teacher wishes to emphasize part of the word, then it can be underlined or printed in red. After discussing a word, the teacher can remove the word and ask the students to spell it by responding either orally or writing it. The word then can be shown again for self-correction. Self-correction is an important principal in learning to spell.

The selection of the words in the spelling lesson is the real key. Whether formal or informal, they tend to fall into the following categories: sight words, phonics rules, and spelling rules.

Sight Words

Sight words are words that the students learn as whole words (no phonics and no rules). These are often high-frequency words like the Instant Words. You will find a list of 600 Instant Words on pages 48–53. They are important because they occur so often in writing and reading. In fact, the first 100 Instant Words account for 50% of all written words.

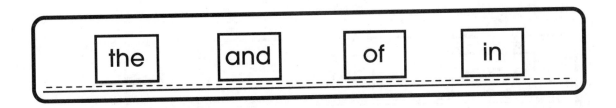

Spelling

Advanced Spelling *(cont.)*

Phonics Rules

Phonics rules explain much about how words are spelled (but not everything). The Phonics Charts on pages 36–47 give you the basic phonics rules. You can use the example words for spelling lessons.

"st" Family

Spelling Rules

Spelling rules help many students to learn to spell better, and they are often woven into more formal spelling lessons, such as those in nearly all major spelling series books. They are also useful in informal spelling lessons when the teacher discovers a particular need. They make excellent supplemental spelling lessons. You will find a number of basic Spelling Rules on pages 54–57. Teach them by putting example words on your pocket chart and showing what happens to the spelling during certain changes, such as adding suffixes.

Adding "s"

Adding "es"

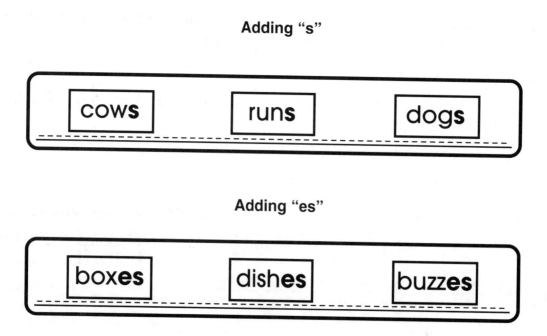

Spelling

Teaching Spelling

Below are some general comments regarding the teaching of spelling.

- Most spelling experts agree that good pronunciation helps learning to spell. Exaggerate enunciation when giving the spelling words. Some teachers introduce the words by pronouncing them syllable by syllable. You may have noticed that often National Spelling Bee champions do that.

- Point out trouble parts of words like silent letters or unusual or nonphonetic parts of words.

- Discuss the meaning and use of each word. Use the word in a sentence when giving the spelling test.

- Vowels cause more trouble than consonants. Stress vowel sounds and the way they are spelled.

- Give students a lot of praise for good spelling, particularly if they are showing improvement. Look at their spelling progress charts regularly.

- Do not let spelling get in the way of good story writing. Let students use invented spelling on first drafts. Later they can proofread and correct.

- Have a little fun. Play some spelling games or have a spelling bee. Laugh at some mistakes, both theirs and yours. Remember that the only people who do not make spelling errors are people who do not write anything.

Traditional Spelling Lessons

1. On Monday give a pretest of all the week's spelling words—about 20 words in upper elementary and less in primary grades.

2. Let students self-correct their papers.

3. Have students study the words that they missed. See the five-step study method on the next page.

4. Give a second trial spelling test on Wednesday.

5. Give the final spelling test on Friday.

For more information on spelling instruction plus weekly lessons, see Dr. Fry's *Spelling Book Grades 1st–6th, Words Most Needed Plus Phonics*, TCM 2750.

Spelling

Five-Step Word Study

1. Look at the whole word carefully.

2. Say the word aloud to yourself.

3. Spell-say each letter to yourself.

4. Write the word from memory. (Cover the word and write it.)

5. Check your written word against the correct spelling. (Circle errors and repeat Steps 4 and 5.)

Writing

Phrases and Sentences

Beginning reading and writing are much more than just learning some picture nouns. Learning single nouns is a useful bit of literacy that we might call "labeling." Teachers sometimes label desks with student names or label objects around the classroom. This is okay, but a more important skill is learning to write phrases and sentences. To do this, you will need "structure words" like the beginning Instant Words and other parts of speech, such as verbs. You will also need to use the teaching techniques like those mentioned in the Basic Reading Lesson (page 9) and Beginning Spelling lesson (pages 15 and 16).

Structure words are the little words that hold the language together. Though they have little direct meaning, they are absolutely necessary for grammar. You cannot write much of anything without them. They are also the most commonly used reading words in the English language.

Here are some of the most common structure words:

the	of	to	in

a	and

And here are some common and easy verbs:

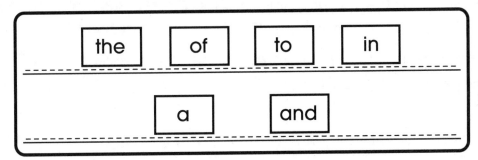

is	was	are	go
like	look	see	write

Using these words and some Picture Nouns, you can write sentences like the following:

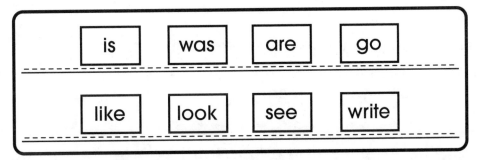

See	the	ball	.

Using Rebuses

You can add an interesting variation to teaching reading and writing by using *rebuses* (picture words) instead of written words. This will allow you to extend the vocabulary into words that are not known in print to the student. It is especially useful with beginning readers and with ELL students who are just learning the English language.

For example, using some of the Picture Nouns on pages 63–82, you can use your pocket chart to make up sentences like the following:

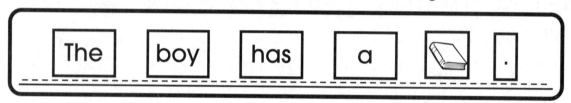

You can make up your own rebus cards by cutting pictures out of old magazines or drawing simple pictures. Or, you can have the students make up their own rebus cards with a picture on one side and the printed word on the other like the *Picture Noun Flashcards* published by Teacher Created Materials.

After you have a reading lesson using some rebuses, you can then turn the cards over so that the students read the printed words.

- **Follow-up 1**

  Let the students self-study a short stack of rebus cards by trying to read just the word side of the card, then self-correct by turning the card over to see the picture.

- **Follow-up 2**

  The students can give themselves a self-administered spelling test by looking at the picture, trying to write the word, then turning the card over to see if it was spelled (written) correctly.

> **Caution:** Rebuses can be a little troublesome because a picture can have several names. For example, a picture of a dog might be called a "wolf," a "puppy," etc. To avoid this, use just one word for a picture in your lesson.

Phonics

Onset and Rime

Many teachers begin phonics instruction with *onset* and *rime*, which are also called *phonograms* or *phonics patterns*. And even if you do not begin with onset and rime, usually later in phonics instruction you will use this powerful and well-researched method.

Basically, this method involves substituting the beginning consonant sound. Pocket charts and individual letter cards can be used for this type of lesson. It is a little easier if you use onset cards that are single consonants or consonant blends, such as *c, b, m,* or *sp*.

Rime cards (phonograms), which are a vowel plus a following consonant, can also be used, such as *-at, -am, -ack,* or *-ill*.

You can use these to put together all sorts of words. For example, in the *-at* family you can make *cat, bat, mat,* or *spat*.

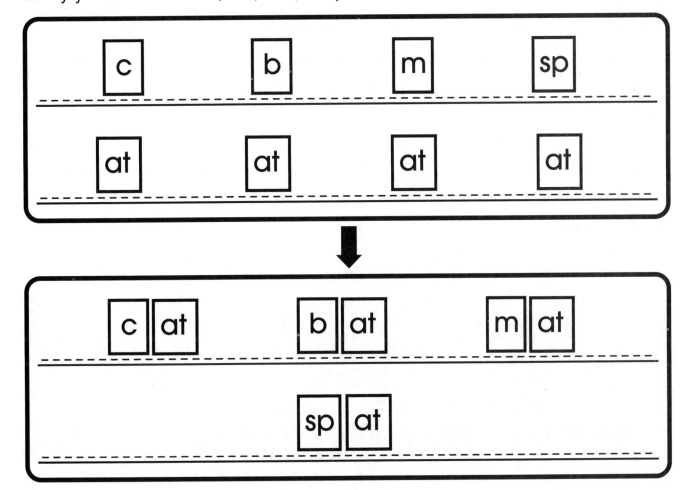

Phonics

Onset and Rime *(cont.)*

In the basic onset and rime lesson, the teacher presents a word and shows how it can be made into a new word by just changing the initial consonant. This shows the student the importance of one letter and that different letters make different sounds. This is the essence of phonics.

On pages 36–38 you will find a list of onset and rime families (phonograms) that you can use to make your own cards, or commercially-made cards are available with the onset on one card and the rime on another card.

- **Variation 1**
  Have a student do the initial onset card substitution and read the new word.

- **Follow-up 1**
  Give the students a phonogram and several consonants and have them write the new words that they make.

- **Follow-up 2**
  The next day, review the combinations taught and add some new ones.

- **Follow-up 3**
  Give a spelling test using just words from one phonogram family.

(*Note:* Dr. Fry's *Phonogram Flashcards* have 31 common onsets on cards and 20 common rimes on cards. These can be put together to generate over 600 words.)

Caution: Your lessons will be more efficient if you preselect just the onset cards (initial consonants) that you include in the lesson. This saves time and the confusion of creating nonsense words.

Phonics

Advanced Phonics

Real phonics, or traditional phonics, teaches the relationship between a *grapheme*—which is one or more letters (like *sh*)—and the *phoneme* or speech sound they make. In other words, *phonics* teaches the relationship between letters and their sounds.

Pocket charts can certainly be used to teach phonics. One basic way is simply to take one word and show how it is composed of different sounds, like the word *hat* (h-a-t). Discuss the word and the sound each letter makes. Let the students say the word and pronounce each phoneme separately.

Next, display other simple words and discuss them. You can use handmade or commercially-made alphabet cards to do this. If you are making your own letter cards, remember that some letters like *s* occur far more frequently than *q*, so you will need more of these letters.

After the students have had some practice with the type of lessons above and have acquired more advanced reading skills, you can advance to a more difficult lesson. An example is to use words that contain a specific phoneme-grapheme correspondence. Here are some words that can illustrate the consonant *t*.

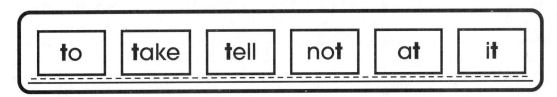

Read the words emphasizing the *t* and pointing to the *t*. Have the students do the same.

For the curriculum contents of all the common phoneme-grapheme correspondences (advanced phonics) and lots of example words, see the Phonics Charts on pages 39–47. These Phonics Charts are also in a suggested teaching order. It is recommended that you teach some easy consonants first, then some short vowels, etc.

Caution: Phonics is important, but do not overemphasize it as it can get boring. Mix phonics in with your other lessons in reading, writing, and spelling.

Grammar

Capitalization

Before very long, the students learn that the first letter of certain words must be capitalized. Of course, if they are rank beginners and doing most of their writing using just capital letters, then this does not apply.

Frequently when beginning to read and spell, just lowercase letters are used. However, the rules of grammar dictate that some words must have the first letter capitalized. Below are the most common instances. For a more complete list of capitalization rules, see page 58.

- First word in a sentence
- Proper nouns: names, dates

- Titles of books and people
- Abbreviations: not all, but most

It is easy to show that the first word in a sentence, a name, or a title must be capitalized. When using lowercase word cards, simply add a capital letter from your alphabet cards to show how the first letter should be changed. Let a student do this when presenting a sentence.

Here are a few easy words that should be capitalized. Present them in all lowercase letters, ask what's incorrect, then show the words properly capitalized.

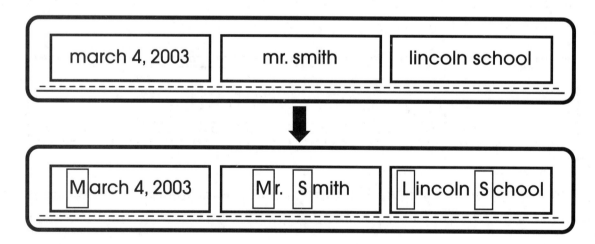

- **Follow-up 1**
  Have the students copy lowercase words, but tell them that they should add capitalization where it is required.

- **Follow-up 2**
  Have students point to the use of capitalization in various written materials like books, newspapers, advertisements, and poems.

Grammar

Punctuation

An important part of writing correctly is to add punctuation marks. Punctuation marks are mostly used to enhance meaning. Often, they indicate *super-segmental phonemes* because they clarify meaning of a larger segment of writing, like emphasizing a word in a sentence. For example, a period means pause at the end of a sentence—the writer is telling the reader, "I have just given you a complete thought unit." Similarly, a comma often indicates a smaller thought unit and a lesser pause. Question marks and exclamation points indicate a change in tone and emphasis. They contribute to "sentence tunes" or the overall sound of the writing, which in turn, adds to the meaning. For punctuation rules and some examples of when they are used, see pages 59 and 60.

Here are the most common punctuation marks: period, question mark, quotation marks, comma, exclamation point, and apostrophe.

When teaching the use of punctuation marks using your pocket chart, make some punctuation mark cards or see page 83. Insert these marks where appropriate in your sentences. For example, the apostrophe mark is used for contractions (See pages 84 and 85 for examples of contractions.). See if your students can insert the punctuation mark in the proper place.

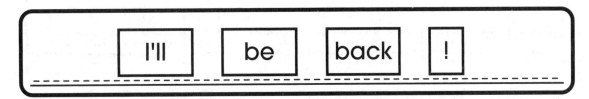

- **Follow-up 1**
  Dictate to your students some short sentences requiring punctuation marks. Make sure they write them using the proper marks.

- **Follow-up 2**
  Give your students sentences to correct by adding punctuation.

Caution: It takes plenty of practice and repeated lessons for students to learn the proper use of punctuation marks.

Morphemes

Morphemes are meaning units. For example, a word is an *independent morpheme*, meaning that it can stand by itself. But smaller meaning units are found within words, and these are called *dependent morphemes*. For example, a prefix is a dependent morpheme and so are both words in a compound word. A compound word also has two morphemes.

Pocket charts are important tools for teaching about morphemes because they can easily show how meaning units in words can be divided or put together. Recognizing common elements of words is very important for learning to read and spell. Learning meaning units (morphemes) contributes to the vocabulary development needed for reading improvement, writing improvement, and for passing many kinds of tests.

Compound Words

You can start your students on the grand morpheme awareness quest by teaching about compound words. One interesting way is to teach compound word families using word substitution as shown below. You can find a list of compound words on pages 86–88.

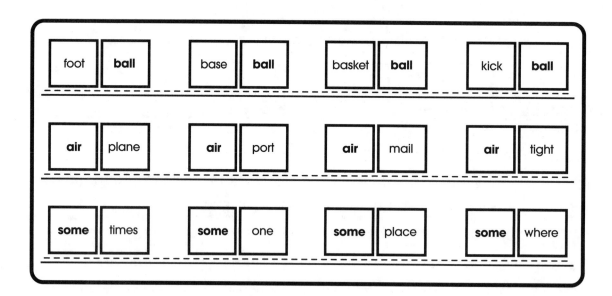

Morphemes

Prefixes

Prefixes are another kind of meaning unit, and they open the door to more upper-level vocabulary improvement taught not just in upper elementary school but all through high school and college.

Prefixes are used frequently on English words that come from the Latin and Greek languages, but the more common prefixes (see the chart below) are often used on words of any origin. We see prefixes in all sorts of combinations, such as those expressing number like the following:

unicycle = 1 wheel   **quad**rangle = 4 sides

bicycle = 2 wheels   **pent**agon = 5 sides

tricycle = 3 wheels   **hex**agon = 6 sides

When using pocket charts for teaching about prefixes, you can use the word-part substitution technique discussed in the previous lesson. Below are a few prefix families. You can find more prefixes and example words on pages 61 and 62. The importance of teaching prefixes is to get the students to seek out word parts to aid in remembering the meaning and spelling of new words.

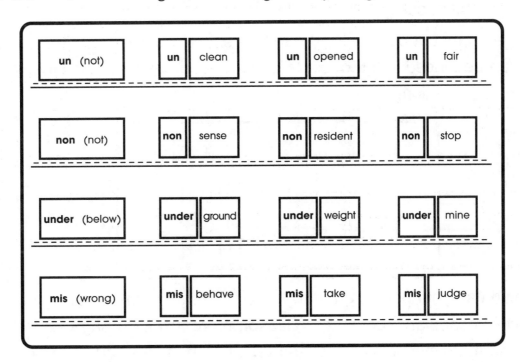

Mathematics

You can use pocket charts to teach mathematics. Below are a few ideas.

- Writing numbers (pages 65 and 73)
- Order numbers by increments: count by 2's, 3's, 5's, etc.
- Reading math symbols, like +, −, =, etc. (pages 89 and 90)
- Displaying math problems

Use your pocket chart to supplement the curriculum in your mathematics textbook. For example, if your textbook uses the symbols > and <, display the symbol cards for them. Cards make numerals and symbols a bit more concrete. An important pocket chart use is to present math problems using your number and symbol cards as shown below.

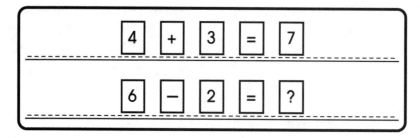

When using pocket charts to teach mathematics, use all your pocket chart teaching skills, such as getting the students involved by letting them place the number cards, make up problems for other students, and try for speed and accuracy in problem solving.

Do not forget that your pocket chart can be used vertically. Use it to show that numbers can be placed in the ones, tens, and hundreds columns when teaching addition and subtraction.

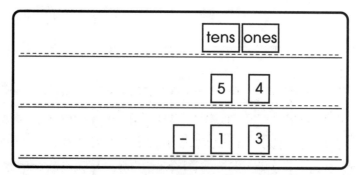

You can also use your pocket chart to teach the reading and spelling of mathematics vocabulary. Look at the lesson on rebuses on page 22, and treat numbers and math symbols as rebuses (see pages 89 and 90).

Grade Levels

Preschool, Kindergarten, and First Grade

Pocket charts readily adapt to all grade levels. It all depends on the type of lesson and your teaching techniques. The content and method can be adapted to fit the age and educational development level of your students.

The following lessons from Section 1 are most appropriate at the preschool to first grade levels or students new to the English language.

- Learning the Alphabet (pages 11 and 12)

- Handwriting (page 14)

- Beginning Spelling (pages 15 and 16)

- Phrases and Sentences (page 21)

- Using Rebuses (page 22)

- Onset and Rime (pages 23 and 24)

- Mathematics (page 30)

(*Note:* The Basic Reading Lesson on page 9 and the suggested variations of it can be used with many of the lessons listed above.)

Caution: Do not assume that older students have mastered all that has been taught in the lessons listed above. Also, do not assume that once you have taught something that it has been learned. Remember to review, review with variation, and review again!

Grade Levels

Grades 2 through 4

The maximum age or grade levels to use pocket charts has certainly been a subject of debate. They have been used to teach foreign languages in middle school and to teach geometry in high school. For this book, we will suggest that for grades two, three, and four, the following lessons would be most appropriate:

- Basic Reading Lesson (page 9)

- Advanced Spelling (pages 17 and 18)

- Advanced Phonics (page 25)

- Capitalization (page 26)

- Punctuation (page 27)

- Compound Words (page 28)

- Prefixes (page 29)

You will find that the charts and word lists in the second section greatly extend the above lessons into the upper grades. For example, the diphthongs and silent letters in the Phonics Charts are certainly not mastered in the primary grades. It takes many pupils well into fourth grade to read all 600 Instant Words, and for some much longer to be able to spell them. The spelling rules are also challenging enough to use all the way through the elementary grades. You will find it necessary to teach and reteach capitalization and punctuation, even in the upper grades. You can also use your pocket chart lessons for just a remedial group or individual students who need help or a challenge.

Caution: Do not try to teach everything everyday with your pocket chart. Keep it as a special teaching tool. Use it for awhile, then put it away. Bring it out later, teaching in another area.

Techniques

General Techniques

Basic Reading Lesson

The Basic Reading Lesson on page 9 is not just a reading lesson. The lesson, the variations, and follow-up suggestions can serve as fundamental pocket chart teaching techniques in many subjects. Let some of the faster students use the pocket chart and cards to help some of the slower students review a lesson.

Word-of-the-Day

When students enter the class, have the Word-of-the-Day up on the chart. This might be a new vocabulary word, a word from a story, or a word from a social studies lesson. Discuss it. Leave it up for awhile. Some teachers use this as a opening activity (i.e., the first thing the students do on entering the class is to write the Word-of-the-Day in their notebooks).

You will find that between making new cards and buying some cards for your pocket chart, you will soon have quite a stack of cards. File them carefully so you can use them for review lessons.

Games

Kids love games. They like to compete to see who can read a word or spell a word first. You can turn over one word in a sentence and see if the students can guess what the missing word is. If you have pairs of words—like a word and its abbreviation, two identical card words, a word and its picture (picture noun)— you can play a Concentration, or match-up, game.

Other Uses

You can do a lot of things with word cards besides sticking them in a pocket chart. You can use them as flashcards for students to review, they can be used for finger tracing, and they can be used for informal tests.

Many of the word lists and charts in this book came from either the book *How To Teach Reading* (TCM 2760) or *The Reading Teachers Book of Lists* by Edward Fry, Jacqueline Kress, and Dona Fountoukidis.

Techniques

Cloze Technique

The Cloze Technique is ideally suited to pocket charts. Basically, it uses a blank space to be filled in by a letter or word.

Phonograms

For example, in using phonograms, the teacher might put up a card with _at on it. The student is given three onset cards (*j, h, x*), only one of which makes sense. The student places the correct card in the blank space.

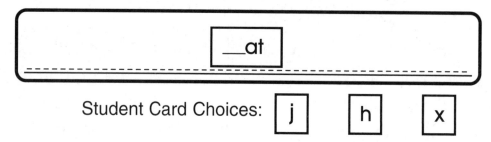

Sentences

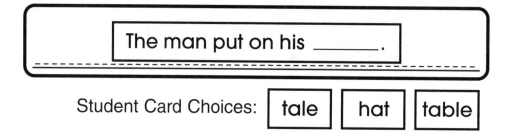

Spelling

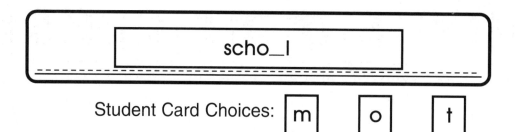

Rebuses

Section 2

Teaching Resources

Phonics Charts

Onsets

Onsets are the beginning consonant sounds in a syllable (or a one syllable word). When put together with rimes (pages 37 and 38), they form common words. See pages 23 and 24 for a further discussion of onset and rime.

Single Consonants

b	**g**	**l**	**r**	**w**
c	**h**	**m**	**s**	**y**
d	**j**	**n**	**t**	**z**
f	**k**	**p**	**v**	

Important Exceptions

c = /s/ before i, e, or y, as in "city"

c = /k/ before a, o, u, as in "cat"

g = /j/ before i, e, or y, as in "gem"

g = /g/ before a, o, or u, as in "good"

ph = /f/ sound as in "phone"

qu = /kw/ blend as in "quick"

(the letter "q" is never used without "u")

Rare Exceptions

ch = /k/ as in "character"

ch = /sh/ as in "chef"

s = /sh/ as in "sure"

Consonant Digraphs

ch as in "church"

sh as in "shoe"

th (voiced) as in "thin"

th (voiceless) as in "this"

wh (hw blend) as in "which"

Silent Consonants

gn = /n/ as in "gnat"

kn = /n/ as in "knife"

wr = /r/ as in "write"

Beginning Consonant Blends

(r family)	(l family)	(s letter)	(s family)	(no family)
br	**bl**	**sc**	**scr**	**dw**
cr	**cl**	**sk**	**squ**	**tw**
dr	**fl**	**sm**	**str**	**thr**
fr	**gl**	**sn**	**spr**	
gr	**pl**	**sp**	**spl**	
pr	**sl**	**st**	**shr**	
tr		**sw**	**sch**	
wr				

Phonics Charts

Onsets and Rimes

Here are some onsets and rimes (phonograms) to use with the methods suggested on pages 23 and 24. Note that the top line in each set has words using only single consonant onsets. The second line in italics has two-letter onsets. Additional onsets and rimes are on the next page.

-ack	back	Jack	pack	tack	sack
	black	*shack*	*track*	*snack*	*crack*
-ag	bag	tag	rag	lag	sag
	brag	*flag*	*drag*	*stag*	*shag*
-am	jam	ham	Pam	Sam	dam
	swam	*clam*	*slam*	*tram*	*cram*
-an	can	fan	man	ran	pan
	than	*plan*	*span*	*bran*	*clan*
-at	cat	bat	fat	rat	hat
	flat	*that*	*brat*	*chat*	*slat*
-ay	say	day	way	may	pay
	play	*stay*	*clay*	*gray*	*tray*
-ell	bell	cell	sell	tell	well
	shell	*spell*	*swell*	*smell*	*dwell*
-ick	sick	Dick	kick	pick	lick
	brick	*chick*	*stick*	*thick*	*trick*
-ill	will	bill	hill	pill	kill
	chill	*still*	*skill*	*spill*	*drill*
-ip	tip	lip	hip	sip	rip
	ship	*chip*	*trip*	*drip*	*flip*

Phonics Charts

Onsets and Rimes (cont.)

These additional onsets and rimes give you further content to work with for your pocket chart lessons. For additional example words for these rimes or for more rimes, see *Phonics Patterns: Onset and Rime Word Lists* by Dr. Fry (TCM 2761).

-ab	cab	dab	jab	lab	crab
-ail	pail	jail	nail	sail	tail
-ain	rain	pain	main	chain	plain
-ake	cake	lake	make	take	brake
-an	pan	man	ran	tan	Dan
-ap	cap	map	tap	clap	trap
-ed	bed	red	fed	led	Ted
-eed	feed	seed	weed	need	freed
-est	best	nest	pest	rest	test
-ew	new	few	chew	grew	blew
-ight	knight	light	right	night	fight
-im	swim	him	Kim	rim	brim
-in	pin	tin	win	chin	thin
-ine	line	nine	pine	fine	shine
-ing	ring	sing	king	wing	thing
-ink	pink	sink	rink	link	drink
-ob	cob	job	rob	Bob	knob
-ock	sock	rock	lock	dock	block
-op	mop	cop	pop	top	hop
-ore	more	sore	tore	store	score
-ot	pot	not	hot	dot	got
-out	pout	trout	scout	shout	spout
-ow	low	slow	grow	show	snow
-uck	duck	luck	suck	truck	buck
-ug	rug	bug	hug	dug	tug
-unk	sunk	junk	bunk	flunk	skunk
-um	gum	bum	hum	drum	plum
-y	my	by	dry	try	fly

Phonics Charts

Easy Consonants

T	N	R
to take tell not at it top	not no new and in can nut	run red read from our for ring

M	D	S
me my mother some from room man	do day down good and said dog	some so see this us yes saw

L	C	P
little like look will girl school letter	can come color because second music cat	put pretty page up jump stop pencil

B	F	V
but be boy about tub remember book	for from first if before off fish	very visit voice give leave have valentine

Phonics Charts

Easy Vowels

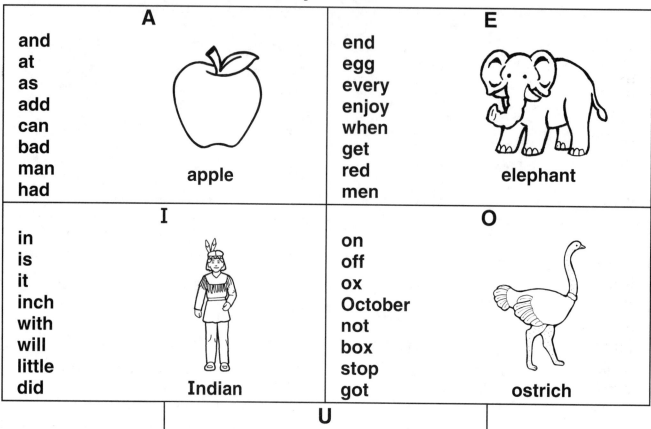

A

and
at
as
add
can
bad
man
had

apple

E

end
egg
every
enjoy
when
get
red
men

elephant

I

in
is
it
inch
with
will
little
did

Indian

O

on
off
ox
October
not
box
stop
got

ostrich

U

up
us
until
under
but
much
just
funny

umbrella

The letter *e* is silent at the end of the word.

    are   **some**

    one   **like**

(These vowels are not long. See page 43 for the final *e* rule.)

The letter *y* sounds like long *e* at the end of a word containing another vowel.

    very   **many**

    any   **pretty**

Phonics Charts

Difficult Consonants

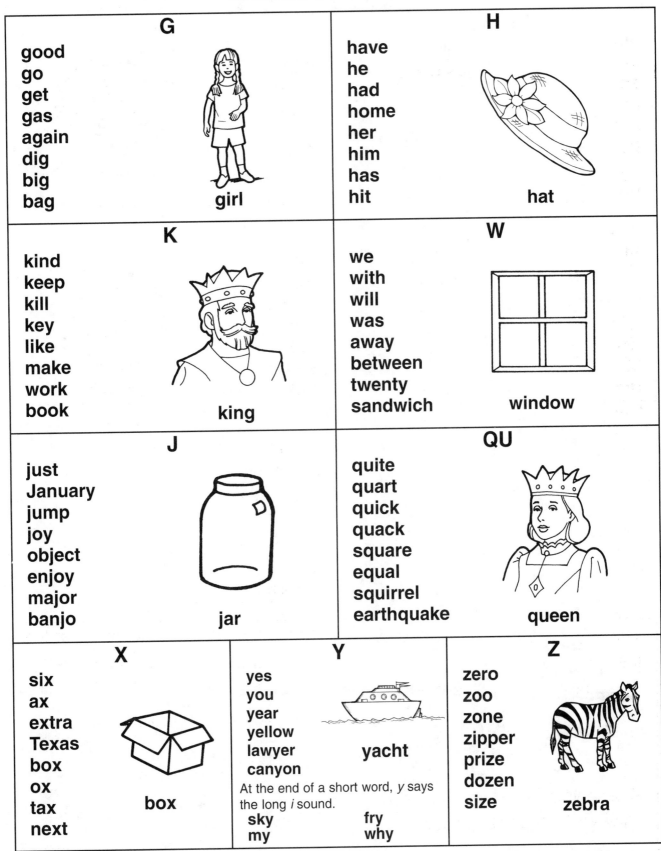

G

good
go
get
gas
again
dig
big
bag

girl

H

have
he
had
home
her
him
has
hit

hat

K

kind
keep
kill
key
like
make
work
book

king

W

we
with
will
was
away
between
twenty
sandwich

window

J

just
January
jump
joy
object
enjoy
major
banjo

jar

QU

quite
quart
quick
quack
square
equal
squirrel
earthquake

queen

X

six
ax
extra
Texas
box
ox
tax
next

box

Y

yes
you
year
yellow
lawyer
canyon

yacht

At the end of a short word, *y* says the long *i* sound.

sky   fry
my   why

Z

zero
zoo
zone
zipper
prize
dozen
size

zebra

Phonics Charts

Consonant Digraphs and Second Sounds

TH (voiced)

the
that
there
then
other
another
smooth
father

mother

TH (unvoiced)

think
thing
thank
third
with
both
fourth
teeth

3

three

CH

child
change
church
chest
which
such
each
teach

chair

WH

when
what
who
wheat
which
where
why
whale

wheel

SH

she
should
shall
ship
wish
wash
fish
bush

shoes

PH (F sound)

physician
phonograph
phrase
photo
alphabet
nephew
triumph
geography

phone

Soft C

(before *e*, *i*, and *y*)

certain
cent
circle
face
once
office
cycle
cyclone

city

S

The *z* sound for *s* never occurs at the beginning of a word.

is
as
was
use
present
please
music

eyes

Soft G

(before *e*, *i*, and *y*)

gem
gentleman
giant
giraffe
charge
age
danger
large

general

Phonics Charts

Long Vowels

Final *e* Rule: An *e* at the end of a word frequently makes the vowel long and the *e* silent. See the examples below. (*Note:* Long *e* is omitted because of its infrequency.)

a-e		i-e	
make	ate	white	time
take	age	while	fire
came	ace	five	nine
made	able	write	mile
name	ape	ride	like
o-e		**u-e**	
home	alone	use	
those	nose	produce	
close	bone	lube	
hope	pole	pure	
note	rose	tube	

#3522 Pocket Charts

Phonics Charts

Long Vowels *(cont.)*

Open Syllable Rule: When a syllable ends in a vowel, that vowel frequently has the long sound.

A	E	I	O	U
A-pril	we	I	so	du-ty
pa-per	be	i-de-a	go	pu-pil
la-dy	he	pi-lot	no	mu-sic
ba-by	e-ven	ti-ny	o-pen	stu-dent
ra-dio		li-on	hell-o	Jan-u-ar-y

Long Vowel Digraphs: These two vowel-letter combinations are called *digraphs*, and they make just one phoneme (a long vowel sound).

AI	AY	EA	EE	OA	OW
fail	stay	eat	see	coat	own
remain	day	year	three	soap	know
train	gray	please	seem	road	show
aid	clay	easy	sleep	oak	yellow
chain	crayon	sea	tree	loan	bowl

Phonics Charts

Schwa and Vowel Plus "R"

Schwa: The unaccented vowel in a word frequently has the sound of *a* as in *ago*.

A	E	O
about	happen	official
again	problem	oppose
away	bulletin	money
several	hundred	canyon
China	united	

The letters *er, ir,* and *ur* frequently all make the same sound.

ER	IR	UR
her	first	turn
were	dirt	hurt
other	third	fur
after	sir	hurry
camera	circus	Thursday

The letters *ar* have two sounds: *ar* as in *far* and *ar* ("air") as in *vary*. The letters *or* have a unique *o* /ô/ sound (broad *o* plus *r*).

AR		OR
/är/	"air"	for
star	library	or
are	vary	before
far	Mary	more
start	care	horn
hard	January	
car	share	

Phonics Charts

Diphthongs and Other Vowel Sounds

Broad *o* sound is made by *o, al, aw,* and *au.*

O	AL	AW	AU
on	all	draw	because
long	salt	law	author
upon	also	awful	August
off	talk	lawn	haul
song	call	straw	daughter

Diphthongs make a sliding sound from one vowel sound to another.

OI	OY	OU	OW
OI and OY make the same sound.		OU and OW make the same sound.	
point	annoy	out	how
voice	enjoy	about	down
noise	toy	our	brown
oil	royal	round	now
boil	oyster	loud	flower

Double *o* and Short *ea*

OO		EA
Double O		**Second Sound of *ea***
long sound	short sound	short *ea* sound
soon	good	dead
school	foot	ahead
too	look	heavy
room	took	ready
zoo	cook	feather

Silent Letters

KN	GH
K before N is silent.	GH is usually silent.
knife	eight
knee	high
know	might
knot	light
knight	right
knit	caught

Consonant Blends

R Family

PR—pretty	prince	prize	April
TR—truck	trick	true	extra
GR—grapes	green	grand	hungry
BR—bread	brick	bring	zebra
CR—crab	cry	crow	across
DR—drum	drug	dress	hundred
FR—frog	free	from	afraid

S Family

ST—stamp	stop	stone	best
SP—spoon	sport	spring	crisp
SC—scout	scrub	screw	scoop
SK—skate	sky	skin	mask
SW—swing	swim	sweep	swell
SM—smile	smell	smoke	smart
SN—snow	snake	snap	snooze

L Family

PL—plate	play	please	supply
CL—clock	class	cloud	include
BL—black	blue	blood	tumbler
FL—flag	flower	fly	snowflake
SL—slow	sleep	sled	asleep
GL—glass	glad	glory	angle

Orphan

TW—twins	twelve	twice	between

600 Instant Words

These are the most often used words in reading and writing. The words are listed in order of frequency. Make sure students know most of these before teaching the second 100. Teach only a few at a time to keep the success rate high. Use these words for flashcards, games, spelling lessons, or just read down the column. These high-frequency words are also called "sight words" because they must be recognized instantly, on sight, for reading fluency.

The First 100 Instant Words

Words 1–25	Words 26–50	Words 51–75	Words 76–100
the	or	will	number
of	one	up	no
and	had	other	way
a	by	about	could
to	words	out	people
in	but	many	my
is	not	then	than
you	what	them	first
that	all	these	water
it	were	so	been
he	we	some	call
was	when	her	who
for	your	would	am
on	can	make	its
are	said	like	now
as	there	him	find
with	use	into	long
his	an	time	down
they	each	has	day
I	which	look	did
at	she	two	get
be	do	more	come
this	how	write	made
have	their	go	may
from	if	see	part

600 Instant Words

The Second 100 Instant Words

Words 101–125	Words 126–150	Words 151–175	Words 176–200
over	say	set	try
new	great	put	kind
sound	where	end	hand
take	help	does	picture
only	through	another	again
little	much	well	change
work	before	large	off
know	line	must	play
place	right	big	spell
years	too	even	air
live	means	such	away
me	old	because	animals
back	any	turned	house
give	same	here	point
most	tell	why	page
very	boy	asked	letters
after	following	went	mother
things	came	men	answer
our	want	read	found
just	show	need	study
name	also	land	still
good	around	different	learn
sentence	farm	home	should
man	three	us	American
think	small	move	world

600 Instant Words

The Third 100 Instant Words

Words 201–225	Words 226–250	Words 251–275	Words 276–300
high	saw	important	miss
every	left	until	idea
near	don't	children	enough
add	few	side	eat
food	while	feet	face
between	along	car	watch
own	might	miles	far
below	close	night	Indians
country	something	walked	really
plants	seemed	white	almost
last	next	sea	let
school	hard	began	above
father	open	grow	girl
keep	example	took	sometimes
trees	beginning	river	mountains
never	life	four	cut
started	always	carry	young
city	those	state	talk
earth	both	once	soon
eyes	paper	book	list
light	together	hear	song
thought	got	stop	being
head	group	without	leave
under	often	second	family
story	run	later	it's

600 Instant Words

The Fourth 100 Instant Words

Words 301–325	Words 326–350	Words 351–375	Words 376–400
body	order	listen	busy
music	red	wind	pulled
color	door	rock	draw
stand	sure	space	voice
sun	become	covered	seen
questions	top	fast	cold
fish	ship	several	cried
area	across	hold	plan
mark	today	himself	notice
dog	during	toward	south
horse	short	five	sing
birds	better	step	war
problem	best	morning	ground
complete	however	passed	fall
room	low	vowel	king
knew	hours	true	town
since	black	hundred	I'll
ever	products	against	unit
piece	happened	pattern	figure
told	whole	numeral	certain
usually	measure	table	field
didn't	remember	north	travel
friends	early	slowly	wood
easy	waves	money	fire
heard	reached	map	upon

600 Instant Words

The Fifth 100 Instant Words

Words 401–425	Words 426–450	Words 451–475	Words 476–500
done	decided	plane	filled
English	contain	system	heat
road	course	behind	full
half	surface	ran	hot
ten	produce	round	check
fly	building	boat	object
gave	ocean	game	bread
box	class	force	rule
finally	note	brought	among
wait	nothing	understand	noun
correct	rest	warm	power
oh	carefully	common	cannot
quickly	scientists	bring	able
person	inside	explain	six
became	wheels	dry	size
shown	stay	though	dark
minutes	green	language	ball
strong	known	shape	material
verb	island	deep	special
stars	week	thousands	heavy
front	less	yes	fine
feel	machine	clear	pair
fact	base	equation	circle
inches	ago	yet	include
street	stood	government	built

600 Instant Words

The Sixth 100 Instant Words

Words 501–525	Words 526–550	Words 551–575	Words 576–600
can't	picked	legs	beside
matter	simple	sat	gone
square	cells	main	sky
syllables	paint	winter	glass
perhaps	mind	wide	million
bill	love	written	west
felt	cause	length	lay
suddenly	rain	reason	weather
test	exercise	kept	root
direction	eggs	interest	instruments
center	train	arms	meet
farmers	blue	brother	third
ready	wish	race	months
anything	drop	present	paragraph
divided	developed	beautiful	raised
general	window	store	represent
energy	difference	job	soft
subject	distance	edge	whether
Europe	heart	past	clothes
moon	sit	sign	flowers
region	sum	record	shall
return	summer	finished	teacher
believe	wall	discovered	held
dance	forest	wild	describe
members	probably	happy	drive

The entire list of 3,000 Instant Words can be found in TCM 2750, *Spelling Book (Grades 1st–6th): Words Most Needed Plus Phonics*, which is available from Teacher Created Materials or at educational supply stores.

Spelling Rules

Spelling rules are sometimes strange and wondrous and often more than a little complex. They mainly have to do with adding suffixes. Most of them are incorporated into elementary spelling lessons as incidental information, not necessarily to be memorized by the student. However, they can help the students to begin to see spelling patterns.

Plurals and "S" Form of Verbs

a. Add "s" to most nouns and verbs.
Examples: cows, runs

b. Add "es" if the word ends in "ch," "s," "sh," "x," or "z."
Example: box—boxes

For words ending in "y"
c. If the word ends in a "y," preceded by a consonant, change the "y" to "i" and add "es."
Example: baby—babies

d. Do not change "y" if a vowel precedes it.
Example: key—keys

e. Do not change "y" if it is in a proper noun.
Example: one Kathy—two Kathys

For words ending in "o"
f. For a few words ending in "o," add "es."
Example: go—goes

g. For many words ending in "o," just adding an "s" is okay because either spelling is correct.
Example: banjos or banjoes

h. If the "o" is preceded by a vowel, just add "s."
Example: radio—radios

For words ending in "f"
i. For a few nouns ending in "f" (or "fe"), change the "f" to "v" and add "es."
Example: leaf—leaves

Other Plurals

a. Some foreign nouns have different plurals.
Examples: alumnus—alumni, index—indices

b. A few English nouns have different plurals.
Example: foot—feet

c. A few nouns do not change for plurals.
Example: deer—deer

d. Symbols form plurals with an apostrophe "s" ('s).
Examples: 2's or ABC's

Spelling Rules

Possessives

a. Add an apostrophe and "s" ('s) to form a possessive.
Example: cow's

b. If a plural word ends in "s," put the apostrophe after the "s."
Example: two heroes' metals

Adding Suffixes

Basic Rule: Just add the suffix (for example: want—wanted, wanting, wants) except as follows:

For words ending in "e"

a. Drop the final "e" if the suffix begins with a vowel.
Examples: rose—rosy; name—naming

b. Keep the final "e" if the suffix begins with a consonant.
Example: safe—safely

c. Keep the final "e" if a vowel precedes it.
Example: see—seeing

d. Drop the final "le" if the suffix is "ly" (no double "l").
Example: able—ably

For words ending in "y"

e. Change the "y" to "i" if "y" is preceded by a consonant.
Example: baby—babies

f. Do not change the "y" to "i" if "y" is preceded by a vowel.
Example: toy—toys

g. Do not change the "y" to "i" if the suffix begins with an "i."
Example: carry—carrying (The suffix here is "-ing.")

For words ending in "c"

h. Add a "k" before any suffix beginning with an "e," "i," or "y."
Examples: picnic—picnicking, panic—panicky

Doubling the final letter

i. Double the final consonant before adding the suffix if:

1. the word has one syllable (or the final syllable is accented).

2. the word ends in a single consonant (except "x"; for example, box—boxing).

3. the word has a single vowel letter.

4. the suffix begins with a vowel.

Example: brag—bragged

Spelling Rules

Adding Suffixes *(cont.)*

Doubling the final letter *(cont.)*

j. Do not double the final consonant (Basic Rule applies) if:

1. the suffix begins with a consonant.
   Example: bag—bagful

2. the vowel has two letters.
   Example: rain—rained

3. the word has two final consonants.
   Example: hard—harder

4. the suffix begins with a consonant.
   Example: bag—bags

5. the final syllable is not accented.
   Example: benefit—benefited

k. If the word has two syllables and is accented on the last syllable, treat it as a one-syllable word.
   Example: admit—admittance

l. If the word has two syllables and is accented on the first syllable, do not double the last letter (back to the Basic Rule).
   Example: equal—equaled

m. The final "l" is kept when adding "ly."
   Example: cool—coolly

Prefixes

Basic Rule: Prefixes never change the spelling, they are just added on the front of the word.

a. Even if it means having double letters
   Examples: misspell, illegible

b. Often the prefixes "ex" and "self" use a hyphen.
   Examples: ex-president, self-help

"EI" or "IE" Rule

Basic Rule: Write "i" before "e," except after "c."
   Examples: chief, believe

a. If the vowel sounds like long "a," spell it "ei."
   Examples: neighbor, weigh

b. There are plenty of exceptions.
   Examples: receive, their, Neil, science, either, leisure

Spelling Rules

Compound Words

Basic Rule: Keep the full spelling of both words. Do not use a hyphen.

    Examples: ear + ring = earring, room + mate = roommate

A more common usage or more specific meaning tends to put two words into a compound.

    Examples: blackbird (one word), black car (two words)

Caution: There is a whole other set of rules that concern spelling that are usually called phonics, which contain rules like the final "e" rule and consonant or vowel digraphs. In addition to this, there is another set of rules for syllable division, which is related to spelling. Besides this, there are many spelling patterns which include affixes and other morphological units, multiple phoneme units of words (like "tion") and phonograms, and relatively rare single phoneme correspondences (phonics) like "dge" making the /j/ sound in "fudge."

It is obvious from all the studies on "invented spelling" that children and most beginning writers and readers do develop their own set of "rules." For example, preschoolers often say "foots" showing that they have developed the basic plural-forming rule. These other sets of "rules" might help children and their teachers to show instances where more accurate and sophisticated rules apply. The number of "exceptions" diminishes as more sophisticated rules are developed, but don't panic. There will still be a large body of "exceptions," and we should keep in mind that learning to spell is a lifelong process.

#3522 Pocket Charts

Grammar

Capitalization Rules

Review these guidelines with your students and provide practice exercises for problem areas. Give "proofreading" assignments to help students become sensitive to the proper use of uppercase letters.

- Capitalize the pronoun "I."
  Example: I often sleep late on weekends.

- Capitalize the first word of any sentence.
  Example: Kittens are playful.

- Capitalize the first word and all the important words in titles of books, magazines, newspapers, stories, etc.
  Example: *The Lion, the Witch, and the Wardrobe* is a very good book.

- Capitalize names of specific people, events, dates, and documents.
  Example: The Fourth of July and Thanksgiving are my favorite holidays.

- Capitalize the names of organizations and trade names.
  Example: Ford Motor Company and General Motors make good trucks.

- Capitalize titles of respect.
  Example: Mr. Cox and Ms. Blake are very nice people.

- Capitalize names of races, languages, religions, and deity.
  Example: Some Spanish people are Catholic and believe in God.

- Capitalize the first word in a direct quotation.
  Example: Ann inquired, "Where is the suntan lotion?"

- Capitalize abbreviations and acronyms, all or part.
  Example: I live in the U.S. on Baker Street.

Grammar

Punctuation Rules

Review these rules with your students and provide practice exercises for problem areas. Give "proofreading" assignments to help students practice the proper use of punctuation marks. Make some punctuation cards for your pocket chart or use the cards on page 83.

Period (.)

1. Use at the end of a sentence.

   Example: The birds will fly home.

2. Use after most abbreviations.

   Example: Mr. Cox lives on Green Avenue.

Question Mark (?)

1. Use at the end of a question sentence.

   Example: Who is he?

2. Use to express doubt.

   Example: He ate 14 doughnuts?

Exclamation Point (!)

1. Use to show strong emotion with a word.

   Example: Great!

2. Use to show strong emotion with a sentence.

   Example: You're the best!

Quotation Marks (" ")

1. Use to show a direct quote.

   Example: She said, "May I help you?"

2. Use to set off a title of a story or poem.

   Example: He read "A Visit from Saint Nicholas."

3. Use to imply sarcasm or someone else's use of a term.

   Example: The "hero" was not at home.

Grammar

Punctuation Rules *(cont.)*

Apostrophe (')

1. Use to show possession.

   Example: Bill's bike was broken.

2. Use in contractions to show missing letters.

   Example: Isn't she pretty?

Comma (,)

1. Use to separate things in a list.

   Example: I need bread, milk, and cheese.

2. Use to separate parts of a date.

   Example: February 22, 2000, is the day my sister was born.

3. Use after the greeting in a friendly letter.

   Example: Dear Gerry,

4. Use after the closing in a letter.

   Example: Sincerely,

5. Use to separate the city and state in an address.

   Example: New York, NY

6. Use to separate a name and a degree title.

   Example: Jenn Stock, M.D.

7. Use in written dialogue between the quotation and the rest of the sentence.

   Example: She said, "Stop it!" "Okay," he replied.

8. Use between more than one adjective or adverb.

   Example: The big, bad wolf scared the girl.

Prefixes

Prefix	Meaning	Examples
anti-	against	antiwar, antisocial, antislavery, antifreeze
dis-	not, opposite	disappear, disagree, disarm, dishonest, discontinue
ex-	former	ex-president, ex-student, ex-athlete, ex-teacher, ex-king
im-	not	impossible, impassable, immobilize, immature, imbalance
in-	not	inaccurate, invisible, inactive, indecisive, independent
inter-	among, between	Internet, international, intermission, intervene, interrupt
intra-	within	intramural, intrastate, intravenous, intranet, intramuscular
micro-	small, short	microphone, microscope, microwave, microbe, microfilm
mis-	wrong, not	misbehave, misconduct, misfortune, mistake, miscount
multi-	many, much	multiply, multicolored, multimillionaire, multitude
non-	not	nonsense, nonfiction, nonresistant, nonstop, nonviolent
over-	too much	overdue, overdo, overpriced, overbearing, overactive
post-	after	postpone, postdate, postscript, postmeridian, postwar

Prefixes

Prefix	Meaning	Examples
pre-	before	prefix, precaution, preamble, prenatal, prelude
pro-	favor	pro-war, pro-American, pro-education, pro-trade, pro-union
pro-	forward	proceed, produce, progress, project, prognosis, prophet
re-	again	redo, rewrite, reappear, repaint, reheat, relive
re-	back	recall, recede, repay, reflect, retract, rebate
sub-	under, below	submarine, subzero, submerge, subordinate, subhuman
super-	above, beyond	superman, supernatural, superior, superpower, supervise
tele-	distant	telephone, telescope, television, telegram, telepathy
trans-	across	transport, transfer, translate, transatlantic, transcribe
un-	not	unhappy, unable, uncomfortable, uncertain, unbeaten
under-	below, less than	underpaid, undercover, underground, underneath, underage

Pocket Chart Cards

These words are intended to supplement the first 300 Instant Words for use in beginning or remedial reading instruction. These words can be made into flashcards with the word on one side only or cards with the word on one side and a picture on the other, or they can be cut out and used in a pocket chart. The printed word or picture (rebus) can be used along with the Instant Words to form sentences and phrases.

100 Picture Nouns (People)

boy	
man	
woman	
baby	

100 Picture Nouns (Toys)

ball	
doll	
train	
game	
toy	

100 Picture Nouns (Numbers 1–5)

one	1
two	2
three	3
four	4
five	5

100 Picture Nouns (Clothing)

shirt	
pants	
dress	
shoes	
hat	

100 Picture Nouns (Pets)

cat	
dog	
bird	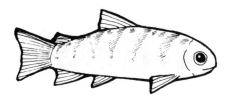
fish	
rabbit	

100 Picture Nouns (Furniture)

table	
chair	
sofa	
chest	
desk	

100 Picture Nouns (Eating Objects)

cup	
plate	
bowl	
fork	
spoon	

100 Picture Nouns (Transportation)

car	
truck	
bus	
plane	
boat	

100 Picture Nouns (Food)

bread	
meat	
soup	
apple	
cereal	Corn Puffies

100 Picture Nouns (Drinks)

water	
milk	
juice	
soda	
tea	

100 Picture Nouns (Numbers 6–10)

six	6
seven	7
eight	8
nine	9
ten	10

100 Picture Nouns (Fruit)

fruit	
orange	
grapes	
pear	
banana	

100 Picture Nouns (Plants)

bush	
flower	
grass	
plant	
tree	

Pocket Chart Cards

100 Picture Nouns (Sky Things)

sun	
moon	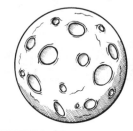
star	
cloud	
rain	

100 Picture Nouns (Earth Things)

lake	
rock	
dirt	
field	
hill	

100 Picture Nouns (Farm Animals)

horse	
cow	
pig	
chicken	
duck	

78

100 Picture Nouns (Workers)

farmer	
police	
cook	
doctor	
nurse	

100 Picture Nouns (Entertainment)

television	
radio	
movie	
ball game	
band	

100 Picture Nouns (Writing Tools)

pen	
pencil	
crayon	
chalk	
computer	

100 Picture Nouns (Reading Things)

book	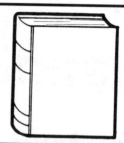
newspaper	
magazine	
sign	
letter	

Punctuation Marks

period	.
question mark	?
exclamation mark	!
comma	,
quotation marks	" "
apostrophe	'

Contractions

I am	I'm
I will	I'll
he has he is	he's
she has she is	she's
it has it is	it's

84

Contractions *(cont.)*

cannot	can't
do not	don't
we have	we've
did not	didn't
they will	they'll

Compound Words

airplane	anybody
anyway	anywhere
backpack	baseball
bedroom	birthday
chalkboard	cowboy

86

Compound Words *(cont.)*

cupcake	doorbell
everybody	everything
football	goldfish
hamburger	homework
inside	newspaper

Compound Words *(cont.)*

notebook	**online**
playground	**popcorn**
strawberry	**sweatshirt**
textbook	**toothbrush**
watermelon	**weekend**

88

Math Symbols

plus	**+**
minus	**–**
times	**X**
divided by	**÷**
equals	**=**

Math Symbols *(cont.)*

is not equal to	≠
is less than	<
is greater than	>
cent(s)	¢
dollar(s)	$

Pocket Chart Cards

Traditional Printing

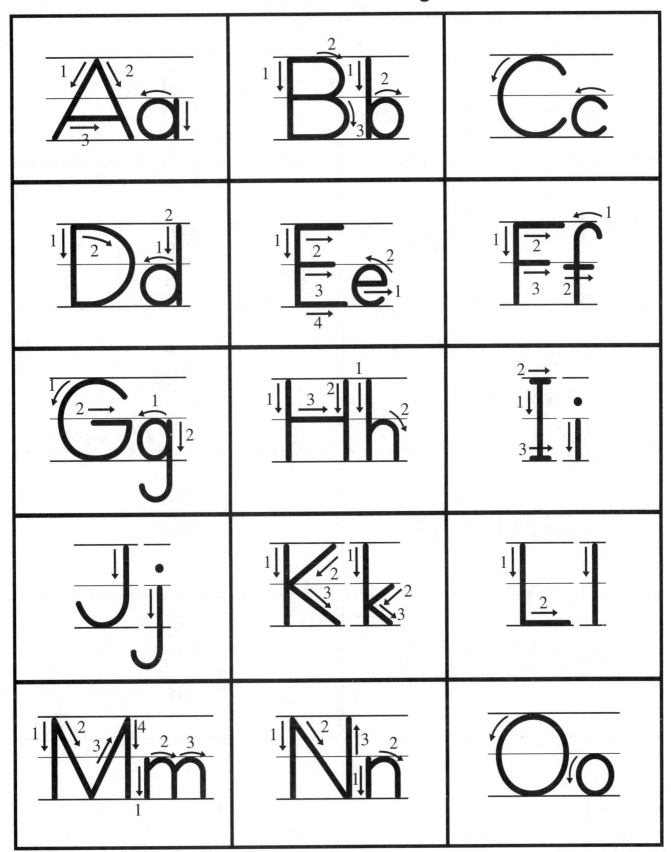

Traditional Printing *(cont.)*

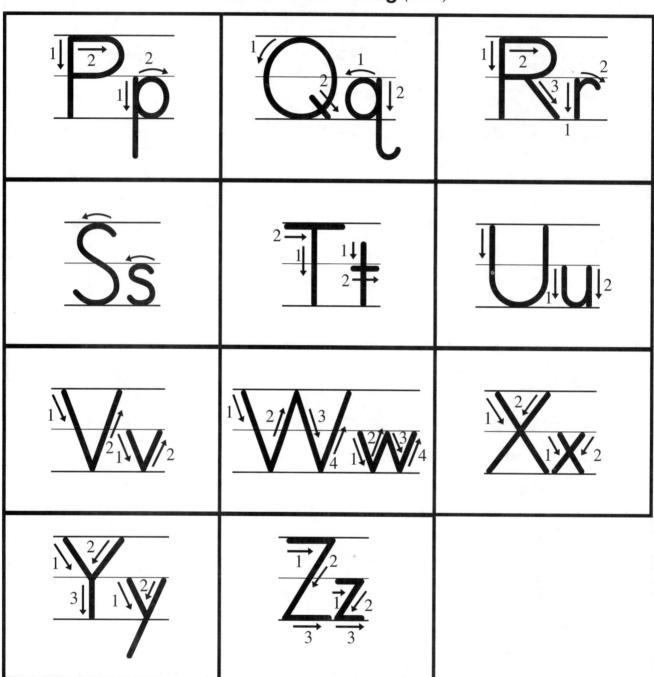

Pocket Chart Cards

Modern Printing

Aa	Bb	Cc
Dd	Ee	Ff
Gg	Hh	Ii
Jj	Kk	Ll
Mm	Nn	Oo

Modern Printing *(cont.)*

Pp	Qq	Rr
Ss	Tt	Uu
Vv	Ww	Xx
Yy	Zz	

Pocket Chart Cards

Cursive Writing

$\mathcal{Aa}$	$\mathcal{Bb}$	$\mathcal{Cc}$
$\mathcal{Dd}$	$\mathcal{Ee}$	$\mathcal{Ff}$
$\mathcal{Gg}$	$\mathcal{Hh}$	$\mathcal{Ii}$
$\mathcal{Jj}$	$\mathcal{Kk}$	$\mathcal{Ll}$
$\mathcal{Mm}$	$\mathcal{Nn}$	$\mathcal{Oo}$

Cursive Writing *(cont.)*

Pp	Qq	Rr
Ss	Tt	Uu
Vv	Ww	Xx
Yy	Zz	